Xenophobe's guide to the IRISH

Frank McNally

*thanks for everything,
Hugo
Do keep in touch
Every good wish,
Janet and
Ian*

Ⓞ

Oval Books

Published by Oval Books
5 St. John's Buildings
Canterbury Crescent
London SW9 7QH
United Kingdom

Telephone: +44 (0)20 7733 8585
E-mail: info@ovalbooks.com
Web site: www.ovalbooks.com

Published by Oval Books, 2005
Reprinted 2006

New edition 2008, reprinted 2009

Editor – Catriona Tulloch Scott
Series Editor – Anne Tauté

Cover designer – Vicki Towers
Printer – J.F. Print Ltd., Sparkford, Somerset
Producer – Oval Projects Ltd.

Xenophobe's® is a Registered Trademark.

ISBN: 978-1-906042-37-0

Contents

The number of Irish in the Republic of Ireland is
4 million, of which 1.3 million live in greater Dublin which is
almost as many as the number of people who live in Northern
Ireland. The combined population is thus around 5.5 million,
compared with 3 million Welsh, 5 million Scots, 20 million
Aussies, 52 million English and 307 million Americans.

The Republic of Ireland is nearly five times the size of
Northern Ireland, but could fit into Florida twice.
However, Northern Ireland and the Republic of Ireland
taken together are a bit larger than Scotland.

Nationalism & Identity

Forewarned

There is a country called Ireland and a state called Ireland, and these are not the same thing. The country called Ireland includes Northern Ireland whereas the state called Ireland once claimed to include it, and now merely aspires to include it, eventually. For the moment, a majority of Northern Ireland's population prefers the status quo (union* with Great Britain, that is, not the 1970s rock band).

You may know Ireland as 'The Republic of Ireland', but this is only a working title. The name of the state is 'Ireland', or in the Irish language 'Eire'. For obvious reasons, the pro-British majority of Northern Ireland dislikes using the term 'Ireland' to refer to the Republic. So although they have no enthusiasm for the Irish language, they often use the term '*Eire*' in English. This is considered an insult by people in the Republic, and is intended as such by Northern Ireland unionists, although both sides would have a hard job to explain why. English people sometimes use 'Eire' without intended insult, which is OK because they don't know any better.

> **❝You may know Ireland as 'The Republic of Ireland', but this is only the working title.❞**

* Which is why they are called Unionists.

1

Many people in the Republic don't like using the term Northern Ireland, because the capital letters make it look too permanent. Depending on how nationalistic they are, they prefer to call it 'the occupied six counties' (extreme nationalist), 'the wee six' (extreme nationalist with folksy sense of humour), 'the north of Ireland' (moderate nationalist), or just 'the North', complete with capital N (liberal, sophisticated, hardly nationalist at all, just making a point). Pro-British northerners also sometimes use the province-name 'Ulster' for Northern Ireland. But Northern Ireland contains only two-thirds of Ulster – the rest is in the Republic, and people there don't like the U-name being misappropriated.

> **❝ Many people in the Republic don't like using the term Northern Ireland, because the capital letters make it look too permanent. ❞**

In short, the country called Ireland is a diplomatic minefield for the unwary. The safest thing is to refer informally to 'the north' and 'the south'. If you speak fast enough, no-one will able to tell whether you're using capital letters. Just remember that the most northerly part of the south – Donegal – is further north than anywhere in the North. Otherwise, the already high risk of getting lost in Ireland (see Road Signs) will be increased unnecessarily.

> **❝ In short, the country called Ireland is a minefield for the unwary. ❞**

The Border

The Republic of Ireland and Northern Ireland are divided by a line known simply as 'the Border'. This may be conspicuous on maps and even in books and newspapers, where it is often given a capital 'B', but it is usually less conspicuous on the ground. You can cross it repeatedly without even noticing (a claim made by the British army when it was caught on the wrong side).

Typically, the Border is marked by nothing more than a stream or bridge. But the line often passes through individual farms, farmyards, and houses. Indeed, thanks to the lucrative fuel-excise differentials between North and South, it even sometimes passes through large diesel tanks, owned by smugglers.

> **The Border is marked by nothing more than a stream or bridge. But the line often passes through individual farms, farmyards, and houses.**

Road signs are usually a reliable indication that you have changed jurisdictions. In the South, direction signs appear – if they appear at all – in both English and Irish; whereas in the North, they're in English only. Post-boxes provide clues too. As in other parts of the U.K., the North has the distinctive red Victorian post-box. The Republic also has the distinctive red Victorian post-box, except that, after independence, it was painted green.

Perhaps the most reliable indicators that you have

crossed the Border are flags. Northern Ireland's rival communities like to display flags and emblems to demonstrate their respective loyalties, and the areas immediately north of the Border are mostly nationalist. So when you're driving northwards and suddenly, everywhere you look, you see the flag of the Republic, you can take it as a certainty you're no longer in it.

The eight hundred years of oppression

Irish history is a long series of invasions, with one notable blip: in a cruel irony, the Romans – whose genius for plumbing could have been useful – decided Ireland was too wet to bother with. Few other marauding armies passed up the opportunity, however, so it was no great surprise when the Normans arrived from Britain in 1169, and launched the Eight Hundred Years of Oppression.

> **❝Irish history is a long series of invasions, with one notable blip: in a cruel irony, the Romans decided Ireland was too wet to bother with. ❞**

Once ensconced, they ignored repeated hints to leave. But as had happened with all previous invaders, the Normans (or the 'Old English', as they became known) were soon assimilated, becoming, in a famous phrase, 'more Irish than the Irish themselves'. This development was regarded with concern back in England, where the New English had become more

Norman than the Normans themselves.

Reconquering Ireland, they imposed Penal Laws which banned a number of popular activities, e.g., 'being Irish'. They also 'planted' new settlers who were more water-resistant than the Normans and less vulnerable to the effects of Celtic mist. The settlers who were introduced to the North of Ireland in the 17th century were assimilation-proof partly because of religion. Whereas the Irish and the Old English remained Roman Catholic after the Reformation, these newcomers were Protestants of two main Scottish types – 'Staunch' and 'Fierce'. Britain's wars of religion came to a head on Irish soil in the battles of the Boyne (1690) and Aughrim (1691), when God lined out for both sides, but apparently fought a bit harder for the Protestants.

> **66 The English 'planted' new settlers who were more water-resistant than the Normans and less vulnerable to the effects of Celtic mist. 99**

By Irish standards, the 18th century was peaceful with only one attempted revolution at a cost of 30,000 or so lives. An indirect cause of this rebellion in 1798 was the Act of Union which made Ireland and Britain a single parliamentary unit. During the 19th century, famine and mass emigration reduced the population of Ireland by half. For those left alive the campaign for Home Rule took on a new urgency.

In 1916 militant republicans had another go.

Unlike all previous uprisings which were marked by unrealistic optimism, the insurgents this time shrewdly calculated they would lose. They even devised a cunning revolutionary concept known as 'the triumph of failure'. The plan was a huge success when the British not only put down the rebellion but shot the leaders, thereby alienating public opinion and swinging it behind the rebels. Independence followed for 26 of Ireland's 32 counties.

66 By Irish standards, the 18th century was peaceful with only one attempted revolution at a cost of 30,000 or so lives. 99

The Protestants in the North – now more British than the British themselves – vetoed moves for an all-Ireland republic and set up their own parliament, loyal to the crown, in Belfast. It was based on the concept of 'one-man, one-vote', but only loosely. Anti-Catholic discrimination was widespread, so that by 1969 – the octocentenary of the Norman invasion – Irish nationalists could officially proclaim themselves victims of Eight Hundred Years of Oppression. They still claim copyright on the term.

(Many northern Catholics still considered themselves oppressed well into the 1990s, earning the title of the 'Most Oppressed People Ever', or MOPE, for short. A few enthusiasts still make the effort to feel oppressed today. However, the term Eight Hundred Years of Oppression has become frozen in time, like a listed building on to which you cannot add an extension.)

Anthems

Like many national anthems, the Irish one is an old-fashioned call to arms against (unnamed) invaders. Out of politeness, however, it is always sung in Irish, so friendly visitors won't understand the words and therefore can't take it personally. Many Irish people don't understand the words either. But this is not usually a problem.

Where the anthem does cause problems is in sports such as rugby, in which Ireland fields an all-island team. Although Ulster rugby players – drawn almost exclusively from the pro-British Protestant community – are even less likely to understand the words, they have always known that the song does not represent their tradition. Eventually the sport's authorities were forced to come up with a neutral alternative.

> **The national anthem is always sung in Irish, so friendly visitors won't understand the words and therefore can't take it personally.**

The result is that at home rugby internationals there are now two anthems: the official Irish-language one about fighting for freedom, and the English-language which also mentions fighting, but of a vague, non-political kind. Luckily, only the latter is played at away fixtures. Otherwise on visits to South Africa, where they also have two anthems, the pre-match ceremonies would last longer than the game.

To use or not to use the B-word

The land masses off the north-western shore of France are known to the world collectively as the British Isles. It's a convenient description, and well-balanced Irish people don't object strongly to it. What they do object to is when foreigners go further and assume that the inhabitants of Ireland may be described – even in a loose sense – as British.

> **British people have a particular habit of referring to the Irish as British, and the Irish are always tuned in when they do.**

This is a big faux pas. About 900,000 Irish people, mostly in the north-east, consider themselves British to one degree or another. The other four-and-a-half million fume at their television sets every time an Irish person or thing is so described. For some, if their lives have any meaning at all, it is that they're not British.

The problem is exacerbated by the fact that transmission of Britain's broadcasting service, the BBC, extends as far as the Republic of Ireland (where, happily, its licence fee does not). So opportunities for insult are frequent. British people have a particular habit of referring to the Irish as British, and the Irish are always tuned in when they do.

They know it's not meant to offend, but the careless application of the B-word feels like an inappropriate touch from a former partner with whom they were enjoying a friendly drink after recovering, through counselling, from a bitter marriage. They may well be steeped in British culture (they get all the newspapers too, although they have to pay for those), and it will always be part of their lives, but they've moved on now, and they'd like people to respect that.

Famous Seamus

There is even a perception in Ireland – based on a combination of careful observation and paranoia – that the B-word is only applied to them when they're successful. The issue is con-fused because, for many Irish, the flight-plan to fame involves an onward connec-tion through, and sometimes a stop-over in, London.

> **"For many Irish, the flight-plan to fame involves an onward connection through, and sometimes a stop-over in, London."**

Baggage problems are inevitable. The Nobel-prize-winning poet Seamus Heaney spoke for a nation when, after being included in an anthology of British poetry, he wrote a poem complaining – this is a very loose interpretation – that the publishers had taken his suitcase by mistake.

How others see them

A popular perception of the Irish is that they're all fiery, freckle-faced red-heads who'll start a fight at the slightest offence (e.g., being called 'British'). The bit about the freckles is accurate enough, but the typical Irish person has brown hair and blue eyes. And while they may be descended from the Celts, a fearless people whose warriors were known to run naked into battle, most modern-day Irish people would think twice before running naked into the bathroom.

The myth of the thick Paddy – once especially popular in Britain – has waned in recent years. But the stereotype of the Irish as a charming-yet-feckless people lingers. They are seen as being ruled by their emotions, incapable of organisation, and uninterested in material things. This has become very useful in business negotiations. The ability to pose as hopeless romantics with no concern for money has been a big factor in making Ireland one of the richest countries in the world.

> **The ability to pose as hopeless romantics with no concern for money has been a big factor in making Ireland one of the richest countries in the world.**

Still, wherever the Irish go, the reputation for 'having the craic' (pronounced 'crack') precedes them, which can sometimes cause problems with drug enforcement agents. People expect them to be talkative and funny and the life and soul of the party. This is especially true in parts of Scandinavia, where conversation between locals is normally frowned upon, and an Irish visitor is an excuse to let the hair down.

There's always an element of performance involved in being Irish abroad. Sometimes it's good to get home again and just be yourself.

Forty shades of green

Some of the most dearly-held images of Ireland – especially for Irish Americans – are severely undermined by the Irish who actually live there.

For example, the classic Irish rural dwelling house is the thatched, whitewashed cottage. Its simple, functional beauty can be seen all over Ireland, but only in postcards, old photographs and paintings in galleries. The actual houses no longer exist. If you do see one, it's probably a themed pub that was built last

> **66 The classic Irish rural dwelling house can be seen all over Ireland, but only in postcards. 99**

week. The houses most rural people live in now are modern bungalows. These come in all shapes and sizes, and perhaps the only characteristic they have in common is being devoid of all visual aesthetic.

Because of the song made famous by Johnny Cash, visitors to Ireland also often expect to see the famous *Forty Shades of Green*. But if they're flying into Dublin, over what James Joyce called the 'snot-green' Irish Sea (make that 41 shades), they may be disappointed. A combination of intensive farming and dubious planning decisions has reduced the number of recognisable shades of green around Ireland's capital to about 15. By the time you read this, several of those may have been re-zoned for development, in controversial circumstances.

> **They apply the term 'Irish' to others without the slightest justification, throwing it around like snuff at a wake.**

It's only when you get out into the countryside that Ireland's reputation as the Emerald Isle is vindicated. The further West you go the greener it gets, at least in the gaps between the newly-built bungalows and holiday homes. The rain only adds to the intensity of the colours. After a summer shower, the hedgerows can be no-warning explosions of verdancy. It is no exaggeration to say that in the West, you will see shades of green you have never, ever seen. But some of these will be the rain-coats worn by visitors.

The Irish empire

At the heart of the Irish world-view is a flagrant double-standard. For even as they complain bitterly about the careless British habit of calling them British, they apply the term 'Irish' to others without the slightest justification, throwing it around like snuff at a wake. The main reason for this is that, although a small and relatively insignificant nation, the Irish believe themselves to be the centre of a global empire: the great Hibernian* Diaspora.

Unlike the Scots, the Irish would never claim grandiosely to be running England. But that's only because they're too busy running America. Emigration to the United States has dried up in recent years, but the groundwork is already done, and at the last count a staggering 45 million Americans claimed Irish descent. This suggests either phenomenal success at breeding (and there is evidence to support this in the size of the Kennedy family), or perhaps more real-istically that, of the wide variety of ancestors from which most Americans can choose, the poor oppressed Irish ones still carry the best social cachet. Either way, the figures explain the sense of ownership the Irish feel towards the U.S.

> **❝The Irish would never claim grandiosely to be running England. But that's only because they're too busy running America.❞**

The next biggest colony is probably Australia, where the Irish would broadly define about a third of the population as 'ours'. Overseas territories also include England, Scotland, and even France, where Gaelic chieftains fled in the 17th century and established wineries that thrive to this day. Charles de Gaulle had an Irish great-grand-mother. There are pockets of the empire in places like

---

* Hibernia is the Roman name for Ireland.

South America (Che Guevara was part-Irish too). And thanks to religious missionaries, not even Africa and India escaped Irish influence. In short, the Irish diaspora is an empire on which the sun never sets.

That said, most Irish people recognise that there are many countries throughout the world completely untouched by their influence, whose people neither know nor care anything about Ireland. And if they're going to be like that, the Irish have nothing to say about them either.

Irish dead or alive

The habit of bestowing Irishness on others is not confined to the living. While the term 'British' can fairly be applied to a Dubliner like Oscar Wilde, who was born and died during British rule and spent much of his career in London, the modern Irish take offence at it on his behalf and confer on him posthumous citizenship of an independent Irish republic. He was sympathetic to the nationalist cause, after all.

> **66 Of the wide variety of ancestors from which most Americans can choose, the poor oppressed Irish ones still carry the best social cachet. 99**

Even those less sympathetic may be claimed, however. Because of intertwined histories, the term 'Anglo-Irish' is often used as a flag of convenience for the disputed dead. But where possible, the famous departed – like football players with dual nationality – will be asked to declare exclusively for Ireland. The Duke of Wellington only escaped because, asked if he considered himself Irish, he famously said that being born in a stable didn't necessarily make you a horse.

How they would like to be seen

There used to be a romantic view of the Irish as a wise, poetic people: poor but proud, soulful, eloquent, stoical in the face of suffering, possessed of an ancient Celtic spiritualism and therefore unmoved by the temptations of worldly wealth or fame.

> **The typical Irishman likes to see himself as uniquely centred, rooted in the soil, indifferent to material wealth.**

The living, breathing Irish always knew this was an impossible ideal to live up to, but even today they don't mind having some of these characteristics attributed to them. The typical Irishman likes to see himself as uniquely centred, rooted in the soil, indifferent to material wealth. Ideally he would also like to be extremely rich. Then he would have a better chance to show everybody how uninterested he is in money.

W. B. Yeats' poem *The Fisherman* expresses his ideal image of Irishness: personified by a 'wise and simple' man, 'who goes/to a grey place on a hill/in grey Connemara clothes/at dawn to cast his flies'. The Irish all want to be that fisherman. But as well as casting their flies at dawn in Connemara, they would like to own one of those enormous deep-sea factory-trawlers that operate off the west coast of Africa. Just as a back-up.

It's not easy living up to the Irish image. There can even be a competitive element to it, as the phrase 'more Irish than the Irish themselves' implies. First used of the Normans, to this day visitors to Ireland sometimes outdo the locals in Irishness.

> **To this day visitors to Ireland sometimes outdo the locals in Irishness.**

The phenomenon of the German or Dutch immigrants who adopt Irish ways is well known. They are attracted by ideas of an unspoilt landscape, a simple way of life, a deep reservoir of Celtic spirituality. Settling in the remote countryside, they grow their own organic food, using only traditional methods. They fight passionately against anything that diminishes the environment. They also find time to learn Irish, and to play the fiddle in the local pub of an evening. Gradually, they may even become witty conversationalists, and can 'have the craic' with complete fluency.

In public, the native Irish regard these newcomers with a certain amount of sympathy, suspecting that they may be suffering from some sort of mental condition. Privately, they experience feelings of inadequacy.

They'd like to think that being born in Ireland would give them a decisive advantage in the discipline of being Irish. But the truth is, it's hard to come up to the standard.

Character

Contrariness

Sigmund Freud once claimed that the Irish are the only race who cannot be helped by psychoanalysis. The Irish don't know what exactly he meant by this, and at the rates he was charging, they were afraid to ask. But the general implication was that Irish people are a mass of contradictions and impervious to the rational thought processes that might resolve them.

> **"The general implication was that Irish people are a mass of contradictions and impervious to the rational thought processes that might resolve them."**

Poet G. K. Chesterton seems to have arrived at a similar conclusion when he wrote:

'The Great Gaels of Ireland are the men that God made mad
For all their wars are merry, and all their songs are sad.'

Chesterton was exaggerating about the wars, which

history suggests were only merry in the loose sense of 'spontaneous', 'conceived under the influence of drink', or 'doomed from inadequate planning'. But he had a fair point about the songs. Even today, no Irish celebration is complete without a rendition of *Danny Boy*, the words of which describe a woman saying goodbye to a war-bound lover, foreseeing her own death before he returns, and looking forward to a time when he can join her in the grave. Of course, not all Irish songs are as cheerful as this.

The truth is that, through centuries of misfortune, the Irish have achieved what Freud would have called a 'catharsis' via music, poetry, story-telling, and other forms of expression for which they haven't had to pay a professor with a psychology degree and a funny accent.

66 No Irish celebration is complete without a rendition of *Danny Boy*. 99

The fact that they were such a mass of contradictions to begin with meant there was never any shortage of material – hence the extraordinary success of Irish writers. James Joyce would have been a boon to the psychology profession if literature hadn't got to him first. But it did, and ever since he died, his body of work has been the subject of analysis by a global army of professors, many of them with psychology degrees and funny accents.

On the other hand, it has been argued that what outsiders see as contradictions in the Irish character are in fact elaborate coping mechanisms evolved to deal with the combined effects the Eight Hundred Years of Oppression and the guilt imposed by a particularly severe form of Roman Catholicism.

For example, visitors sometimes notice that the ability to talk, for which the Irish are world-famous, does not always equal an ability to communicate. But the mistake here may be theirs for assuming that the locals are in fact trying to communicate (see Road Signs).

> **"The ability to talk, for which the Irish are world-famous, does not always equal an ability to communicate."**

Creative ambiguity is an Irish art-form, producing such masterpieces as *Finnegans Wake* (1939) and the Good Friday Agreement (1998). Even *Danny Boy* is an example. Musical scholars have argued that the singer of the song could be any one of ten different persons, including mother, father, lover of either gender, priest, or chieftain. The ambiguity of the lyric is quintessentially Irish, as is its sentimentality. And the fact that the words were written by an English lawyer who never set foot in Ireland is just typical of bloody-minded Irish contrariness.

The luck of the Irish

Nowhere is Irish contrariness more evident than in the fact that they consider themselves lucky. 'The luck of the Irish' has become a global by-word for good fortune, despite the fact that Irish history is dominated by war, famine, mass emigration and poverty. It is possible that the earliest users of the phrase were being sarcastic. More likely they were the Irish who emigrated to America in the mid-19th century and arrived there alive, which would explain why they felt lucky. But the irony got lost somewhere, and the concept of Irish luck being a good thing has lodged in the national psyche.

Sodom and begorrah

On the other hand, nearly everything ever said or written about the Irish is currently up for review, thanks to the economic boom that is transforming the country beyond recognition. The land of saints and scholars has become a land of limousines and lap-dance parlours. Most of the emigrants who once sang sentimental songs about the old country are now back living in it, complaining about the traffic and the house prices. The new Irish go to New York for weekend shopping trips, rather than in the hope of a better life.

❝ Nearly everything ever said or written about the Irish is currently up for review. ❞

The sense of dispossession that was central to the Irish mindset for centuries is becoming impossible to sustain, although people still try. In what can only be nostalgia for the misery of the past, the Republic of Ireland's soccer fans celebrate by singing *The Fields of Athenry*, a song that describes the loneliness of a young woman whose husband is transported for stealing corn to feed their children during the potato famine of the 1840s.

> **" The sense of dispossession that was central to the Irish mindset for centuries is becoming impossible to sustain. "**

The luck of the Irish suggests that things will turn out badly in the end. But if the unthinkable happens, and peace and prosperity continue indefinitely, it's bound to have a dramatic effect on the Irish personality. Those now aged under 25 are probably the first generation in Ireland to be free of either religious or colonial oppression, or even of post-colonial guilt. Needless to say, this is a crippling burden. It would be no surprise if this was also the first generation to respond successfully to psychoanalysis.

The Craic

The quintessential Irish word 'craic' is not Irish at all. It was born in England sometime back in the Middle Ages, and was still spelt 'crack' when it crossed the Irish Sea. Nobody knows why it left home. Maybe it felt underappreciated by the straitlaced English. At any rate the term found itself so much in demand in

Ireland that it stayed.

Like the Norman invaders it gradually went native, adopting the Irish dress and accent, and finally even – sometime in the 1990s – the gaelicised form of its name. So successfully has it passed itself off as one of the locals that most Irish people now have no idea it's foreign.

66 **In theory at least, a community of teetotal Trappist monks could 'have the *craic*' without leaving the monastery or breaking any of its vows.** 99

The spelling may be phony, but the concept it has come to describe is central to the Irish character. In its simplest form, craic means conversation, although the term can refer both to the conversation and to the conversationalist. Indeed, to be deemed 'a good craic' is a high honour among Irish people, denoting a sense of humour and a comfortably-furnished mind, as well as an ability to talk at some length without boring the arse off the listener.

In its impersonal form, however, the meaning of craic goes way beyond conversation. It can describe, for example, an atmosphere – especially of the kind found in a good pub. But the craic is not dependent on alcohol any more than it is dependent on conversation. In theory at least, a community of teetotal Trappist monks could 'have the craic' without leaving the monastery or breaking any of its vows. Where the monks might have to draw the line is with the term's third layer of meaning – devilment or mischief. In this sense, the craic is an anarchic tendency in the national psyche. Irish people will do something 'for the craic' when no other logic can possibly justify the action. It can be a small thing, like wearing odd socks, or a medium-sized thing like setting fire to the newspaper of the man next to you on a bus. Not infrequently it ends up in court.

The possibility that the craic is a motivating factor should always be borne in mind by historians, psycho-analysts, and others attempting to explain events that are otherwise inexplicable. Some of the merry wars G. K. Chesterton wrote about may have been started for just this reason. Likewise, Freud's inability to make progress with his Irish patients may stem from his failure to understand that there are three parts to the Irish psyche: the conscious, the sub-conscious, and the bit that does things for the craic.

> **❝ There are three parts to the Irish psyche: the conscious, the sub-conscious, and the bit that does things for the craic. ❞**

Unlike shamrock, the craic can thrive anywhere in the world. It is kept alive like the Olympic Flame, and the torch is handed on wherever the Irish meet. They have no choice in this. When abroad, many of them avoid each other like the plague. But whether they like it or not, they're always running into other Irish people, and the next thing you know, they're having the craic.

It would wear you out, sometimes.

Broadly speaking, craic can be either 'good' or 'great', but when it's really, really good, it is usually said to be 'ninety'. Although nobody knows where this term came from, it has been immortalised in at least one modern Irish ballad, *The Crack was Ninety in the Isle of Man* (written before craic underwent its name-change).

> **The Irishman worries that his neighbour may be 'losing the run of himself'; or worse, that he has already lost it.**

The 'ninety' might be a vague reference to temperature, or to speed. Either way, it is the only precise measurement ever applied to the subject. And although it's acknowledged that the craic can often fall a long way short of ninety, paradoxically, the concept of 'bad craic' does not exist. For the Irish, a person or a thing is either good craic, or no craic at all.

Behaviour

Losing the run of yourself

The typical Irishman worries a lot about his neighbour. Specifically, he worries that his neighbour may be 'losing the run of himself'; or worse, that he has already lost it. This phrase is only ever used in a negative sense, when the neighbour's possession of the run of himself is under threat; so it's hard to define what exactly having the run of yourself entails. But in a very general sense, it means knowing what really matters, staying in touch with your roots, living in harmony with your environment, and so on.

The economic boom that transformed Ireland in recent years greatly increased the danger of the Irish losing the run of themselves. Your neighbour is especially at risk. When he buys a big new off-road vehicle, for example, even though you know for a fact that he never leaves the city, he is in definite peril of losing the run of himself. When his wife suddenly appears to have much larger breasts than she had the last time you looked, she may be losing the run of herself too. And when the pair of them head off to Marbella for Easter, and they only just back from a skiing holiday in Austria, you just know they've lost the run of themselves altogether.

The risk of your neighbour losing the run of himself increases in proportion to how much more money than you he has.

> **66 The risk of your neighbour losing the run of himself increases in proportion to how much more money than you he has. 99**

Luckily, in the reverse situation the problem does not arise. No matter how well off you become, you'll never forget what really matters. It's the others you need to worry about.

This should not be seen as mere begrudgery. It's like

an extension of the Neighbourhood Watch system, where the national soul – rather than simply the security of the neighbourhood – is at stake. While others lose touch with what's really important, you're willing to take on the responsibility of remaining grounded. Because you care.

> **In their weaker moments, the Irish can succumb to straightforward begrudgery.**

Even so, sometimes you fear it's a losing battle: like when you read that a top Dublin department store now has a six-month waiting list for the latest Hermes handbag. At times like this, you will either succumb to despair; or, if you can summon up the energy, you'll write a letter to the newspapers to complain that "We, as a nation, are losing the run of ourselves." The generous use of the term 'We' is disingenuous: the person using the phrase is invariably disassociating himself from the run-loss in question.

Begrudgery

In their weaker moments, the Irish can succumb to honest, straightforward begrudgery. 'It's far from that you were born' is a popular phrase on such occasions, used to remind those who have achieved wealth or fame that you can remember them when they didn't have 'an arse in their trousers'.

Unlike the Americans, who believe everybody can

make it if they work hard, the Irish fear that success may be a limited commodity, like beach-front property, and that somebody else's share may diminish your chances of getting a piece.

The fall of the once-mighty is celebrated in most cultures, but the Irish are particularly enthusiastic. 'Put an Irishman on a spit, and you'll always find another Irishman to baste him,' said George Bernard Shaw. On the other hand, you don't have to have been successful in Ireland to be thought badly of. Another writer, Samuel Johnson, was impressed by the democratic nature of begrudgery in Ireland. 'The Irish are a fair people,' he wrote. 'They never speak well of one another.'

> **" The Irish fear that success may be a limited commodity, like beach-front property. "**

Charm

The charm of the Irish is legendary. The warm smiles, the easy laughter, and the ability to talk all day about nothing are much admired. The mellifluous accents of Cork and Kerry and Donegal only add to the effect.

Thanks to their constant exposure, the Irish themselves don't notice it. But charm is one of their most important exports. And although nobody has ever quantified its contribution to the economy, it must be considerable. Only the charm of Irish negotiators, for example, explains the record per capita financial transfers they secured from the European Union in the two decades after joining. Admittedly this was part of an exchange deal whereby the Irish agreed to help redress Europe's personality deficit. But it was still generous.

> **" The Irish have been taught from an early age to say no, and to relent only after persuasion. "**

The ability to beguile a competitor is an important skill in Ireland, whether you're a horse-dealer or a venture capitalist. Visitors can be disarmed by the smiles and the apparently easy-going approach. It's worth bearing this in mind when negotiating any situation with the Irish. And remember, when you've finally shaken hands on the deal, always count your fingers afterwards.

Why the Irish never say yes

In China, they say yes to everything because it's rude to say no. In Ireland, it's the precise opposite. Offered anything from tea to a seat on the bus, the Irish have been taught from an early age to say no, and to relent only after persuasion. Equestrian show-jumpers may get three faults for a refusal. But for everyone else, it's considered a sign of good breeding.

Offers of hospitality, in particular, must always be tested for their sincerity. In rural parts, this process traditionally begins at the door. A visitor, however familiar, will initially decline the offer of a seat with a phrase such as: "No – I'm not staying." He will then stand in or close to the doorway until at least the third or subsequent offer of a chair, which may have to be pushed across the floor in his direction before he accepts.

> **A visitor, however familiar, will initially decline the offer of a seat with a phrase such as: "No – I'm not staying."**

Once seated, the process begins anew. "You'll have a bite to eat," the host will say. The polite answer to this, whether true or not, is: "No I won't – I'm only up from the table." And so it goes. Even the offer of a cup of tea should be refused until, as a compromise, the visitor offers to take it "in my hand".

This is usually the signal for the host (or hostess, more likely) to fetch out the best table cloth and china, and start making sandwiches. But even after the visitor is ensconced at the table – and he should never get there within the first ten minutes of the visit – he will continually urge the hostess "not to go to any trouble".

Depending on circumstances and time of year, the visitor may be offered "something stronger". To which he should say: "Oh God, no!" Whereupon the host will coax him to have "a small one", and they're off again. It's no wonder political negotiations in Ireland can go on for years.

Implicit in this system is that the good host will not

take no for an answer, unless it's a particularly vehement no, and maybe not even then. The custom was lampooned in the British-Irish sitcom *Father Ted*, in which the priests' housekeeper Mrs. Doyle browbeats all-comers into accepting tea with her relentless mantras: "Ah go on", and "You will, you will, you will." Mrs. Doyle is an exaggeration of an Irish type, but only slightly.

Why the Irish never say no

Despite being brought up to say no to everything, the Irish are fiercely reluctant to complain about things. In restaurants, the word 'no' often disappears from their vocabulary altogether. A waiter will ask "Is everything all right?" And even if the soup is cold, and the white wine is warm, and the Chicken Kiev looks like debris from a nuclear disaster, they still hear themselves saying: "Grand, thanks."

> **Complaining is a national pastime, but only after the fact and never to the person who gives rise to the complaint.**

It's not that they don't like complaining per se. Complaining is a national pastime, in fact, but only after the fact and never to the person who gives rise to the complaint: the rude waiter, the obnoxious shop assistant, or the bank official who makes taking your money seem like a personal favour.

It is yet another national paradox that, despite their reputation for being fiery and rebellious, the Irish can be shamelessly deferential to authority. Maybe this is another of the things that Freud was getting at, when he said they defied psycho-analysis. The Irish bottle up their grievances rather than deal with them. And when they have enough grievances saved up, they either go mad or they write a book. Every so often they get the pike out of the attic and march on Dublin.

> **"The Irish bottle up their grievances. And when they have enough saved up they either go mad or they write a book."**

Road signs

The Irish road-sign system has many of the same qualities as Irish everyday speech. As with the latter, it is not always meant to communicate. In many parts of Ireland, the system seems to be designed to prevent good quality information on the whereabouts of the nearest town from falling into the wrong hands.

Sometimes this will be achieved through the simple absence of signs. Drive into parts of rural Ireland and, like silence falling on a pub when a stranger enters, you'll notice that road-signs are suddenly conspicuous by their absence.

More often, road junctions will drop hints – sometimes playful, sometimes cryptic. They may even give you a sporting chance. A common phenomenon at country cross-roads is a signpost identifying three directions, but not the fourth. The unsignposted road is like the mystery prize in a game show. It might be your intended destination. It might not. You can either go with what you have already, or you can take a chance.

> **A common phenomenon at country cross-roads is a signpost identifying three directions, but not the fourth.**

A benign interpretation of the Irish road-sign system is that it is a conspiracy by the tourist industry to force visitors into asking directions from locals, who will then charm them with their loquaciousness. At any rate, the sign-posts are proven conversation pieces. That's why many of them are missing. They've been spirited off to Irish pubs in New York and San Francisco, where they stand, pointing nowhere in particular, but providing the perfect back-drop for nostalgic conversations about 'the old country'.

Language

Ireland is officially bilingual, with both Irish and English recognised by the Constitution. In fact Irish is exalted as the first official language, English only second. This is not reflected in actual practice, however. Irish is the family china of modern Ireland. It is highly valued, and displayed prominently, usually in a formal setting. It may be brought out every so often for special occasions. But it's definitely not for everyday use.

> **Irish-speaking areas are under more threat than the polar ice-caps.**

The sad fact is that in most of the country Irish is hardly spoken at all. Once the native tongue, its currency is now confined to a few shrinking areas of the West known as the 'Gaeltacht'. These are a bit like the Indian reservations of North America, except that the natives don't get to make their own laws (at least not officially).

Pessimists fear the Gaeltacht is doomed in the long run. And certainly, despite a range of government supports, the Irish-speaking areas are under more threat than the polar ice-caps. Every year a few more pieces melt, break off, and drift away into the rising ocean that is English.

Irish is part of the Celtic family of languages – a twin sister to Scots Gaelic and a distant cousin (they're barely on speaking terms, in fact) of Welsh and Breton. Its grammar is complex and sophisticated, which may be one of the reasons why generations of the Irish studied it every day of their school-going lives without achieving fluency.

The latest attempt to revive it is the growing number of voluntary schools that teach everything through the medium of Irish (including English). An apparent by-product of this movement has been a generation of young female Irish broadcasters who are conspicuously (a) bilingual and (b) good-looking. Nobody claims there's a direct connection, but the phenomenon threatens to make Irish sexy again for the first time since the 16th century.

> **"One initiative was to ban English translations from road-signs and place-names in the Gaeltacht."**

Meanwhile, state policy on the language continues to be controversial. One initiative was to ban English translations from road-signs and place-names in the Gaeltacht. Signs are bilingual elsewhere in the Republic, and critics claimed that Irish-only signs would confuse tourists. Against this it could be argued that, language apart, the Gaeltacht signs follow the same principles as road signs everywhere else. So it won't matter that tourists don't understand them, because they're probably lost already.

Hiberno-English

Most people in Ireland still have the 'cupla focal', i.e., a few words of Irish. These can come in handy on occasion. For example, many Irish find the term *'raimeis'* (pronounced raw-maysh) more expressive than 'nonsense' for describing the sort of, well, *raimeis* that some people speak.

But even where it's never spoken, Irish exists in ghost-form, lurking in the shadows behind what is known as Hiberno-English. Hiberno-English is the dominant dialect in Ireland, and many expressions that seem quaint or eccentric to outsiders are in fact unconscious translations from idioms in the old language. An example is the common Irish greeting: "Is it yerself?" or "Is it yerself that's in it?" To the uninitiated, this may sound like an existentialist reflection on the unreliable nature of identity. In fact, it means "Hello", more or less.

> **There are times when not even death can persuade them to use the past tense.**

Due to irreconcilable differences between Irish and English grammar, the word 'after' is frequently deployed in Hiberno-English. So instead of using the past tense "I've just had dinner", many Irish people will use a convoluted present: "I'm after having dinner". There are times when not even death can persuade them to use the past tense. Thus it's still common to say of someone long-deceased: "She's dead this 20 years", as if it's a condition that could yet be reversed.

When you complain to an Irish person about the weather, or the cost of living, or whatever, you may be told: "Don't be talking!" This is not an appeal for silence. On the contrary, it's just a form of agreement, like "Amen". It indicates that what you said is so self-evidently true that you needn't have said it, although you're perfectly welcome to continue saying it, and at as great a length as you want.

Even the Irish accent is largely explained by the old language. Irish people often use vowel and consonant sounds that don't exist in English but do in Irish. The native tongue may also account for why the Irish often add a syllable to certain English words like 'fillum' (film), where the single syllable sounds lonely on its own.

> **66 There's no use denying it, Irish people talk a lot. They don't know why. It just seems to pour out of them. 99**

A small but classic example of Hiberno-English involves the prepositions 'of' and 'on'. In Ireland things traditionally happen 'of' a given day rather than 'on' it, as in this example, Q: "What did Paddy die of?" A: "He died of a Tuesday."

Conversation

The gift of the gab

There's no use denying it, Irish people talk a lot. They don't know why. It just seems to pour out of them. Maybe it's something to do with living on a lonely mist-covered island on the western fringe of Europe. Whatever the reason, they just can't abide silence. It's a vacuum that must be filled.

Some of the reason is political. For much of their history, the ability to talk was the only thing the Irish had. The very word 'blarney' (meaning gift of the gab) originated in the epic verbal delaying tactics of a chieftain as he attempted to prevent his Blarney Castle falling into the hands of the English in 1602 using nothing but long speeches.

> **66 The urge to self-expression is common among long-colonised peoples, who need to assert their identity. 99**

But tactics apart, the urge to self-expression is common among long-colonised peoples, who need to assert their identity. Having one of the world's longest experiences of colonisation, Irish people need to express themselves at length.

Terms of abuse

The way terms of abuse are awarded in Ireland is a mirror image of the hierarchical structures of freemasonry. In both cases your status (as a mason or an object of opprobrium) will be communicated by a system of secret codes and gestures. The difference with the verbal abuse system is that the communication, and your status in the heirarchy, will usually be known to everyone except you.

The normal entry level is to be termed an 'Eejit'. This implies foolishness, but it has the saving grace of acknowledging that you can't necessarily help being a fool. The stress in the word 'eejit' is on the first sylla-ble, and the amount of stress indicates how big an eejit you are. But as you annoy more and more people, adjectives will be added. Thus, being described as a 'Fierce Eejit' or a 'Buck Eejit' carries the implication that you are in some way contributing wilfully to your condition.

> **66 Being described as a 'Fierce Eejit' or a 'Buck Eejit' carries the implication that you are in some way contributing wilfully to your condition. 99**

After an unspecified period as an eejit, you will probably find yourself promoted to a 'Fecker'. (This is an Irish variation of a popular English word, but the vowel change allows it to be used in more-or-less polite conversation.) Being a fecker implies a certain maliciousness in your character, although the associ-ate rank of 'Ignorant Fecker' suggests that the way you were brought up, you couldn't have been any better.

The next step up is 'Gobshite'. A single disagreeable act may result in you being conferred with this title. But normally the rank is achieved only through hard work over a long period. Again, further adjectives ('Thorough', 'Ignorant', 'Out-and-out') may be added according to merit.

The top echelon in the freemasonry of abuse is a hierarchy all of its own. Admission to this select group is normally at the level of 'Bollocks' (or in the Dublin variant 'bollox'). Once you are dubbed a bollocks, it is then a straightforward ascent though the ranks: you become a 'Big Bollocks', an 'Ignorant Bollocks', and so on, until you reach the penultimate level: a 'Complete Bollocks'. There is only one step up from here, and few people can aspire to achieve it.

Such is the nature of the Irish abuse system, you may have no inkling that you have climbed through the ranks. It is just possible, however, that when you have made it to the very top, somebody (possibly with drink on him) will formally congratulate you on your achievement in becoming a 'Bollocks of the Highest Order'.

A way with words

Apart from the sheer volume of words they produce, the Irish are also noted for the eloquence of their speech. The colourful phrase just comes to them naturally, like whiskers to a goat.

Part of the explanation is their mother tongue. The old language had a rich stock of blessings and curses, often very elaborate. There

> **"The colourful phrase just comes to them naturally, like whiskers to a goat."**

was a poetic phrase for every occasion, from "May the road rise to meet you, and the sun be always at your back" to "That I may live long and have my eyesight and never see hide nor hair of you again".

Even if the phrases are no longer used, the instinct to embellish remains. Exaggeration is an Irish speciality, whether it's: "My neighbour talks so much you'd be hoarse listening to her" or "I'm so hungry I could eat a baby's arse through the bars of a cot". But the meaningful understatement is popular too, especially about alcohol. "He's a great man for the drink" signifies that the man in question is a raving alcoholic, more or less; while "circling over Shannon" is one of the many euphemisms for drunkenness (derived from an occasion when the visiting Russian president Boris Yeltsin had to be sobered up during an extended approach to Shannon airport).

> **Even if the phrases are no longer used, the instinct to embellish remains. Exaggeration is an Irish speciality.**

Another talent is the use of irrelevant detail for adding force to an insult, e.g: "A bigger bollocks never put his arm through a coat!" For some reason, the Irish have a particularly rich reserve of verbal insults. Mean people attract many of them. A person who is tight with money could "mind mice at a crossroads". He would "peel an orange in his pocket". He'd be "afraid to sneeze in case he'd give something away". He probably "still has his communion money" (celebrated in childhood, the ceremony often involves receipt of monetary gifts). He could "live in your ear and rent out the other one".

Feebleness and stupidity are well covered too. A person may be "away with the fairies" (deranged); "as thick as two short planks" (stupid); "soft in the head" (away with the fairies); "brilliant but useless, like a lighthouse in a bog" (excessively gifted, in an academic way), or "as useful as tits on a bull" (not very useful).

While normally in the mood to elaborate, the Irish can say a lot with a single word. After all, 25 years of violence in Northern Ireland was called 'the Troubles', and World War II is still officially known in the Republic as 'the Emergency'.

> **While normally in the mood to elaborate, the Irish can say a lot with a single word.**

A happy Irish person will invariably describe himself as 'grand'. A man who can be trusted is said to be 'sound'. A woman slightly rough in appearance or manners is 'mountainy'. (If emphasis is needed, the word 'out' can be added as a suffix, as in 'grand out', 'sound out', 'mountainy out', etc.)

A person who may be a couple of slates short of a full roof can be said simply to have a 'want'. In their declining years, the Irish go through a series of physical stages during which they may be described as 'failed' (not as well as before), 'shook' (not well at all), and 'bet' (nearly dead).

Greetings

Visitors to Ireland may mistake casual greetings for inquiries after their health. The confusion arises because complete strangers will greet you with the phrase "How're ya?" which sounds like, and indeed is, a question. But it's important to remember that in Ireland a question is not always intended to elicit information.

> **❝It's important to remember that in Ireland a question is not always intended to elicit information.❞**

Yet another consequence of the Eight Hundred Years of Oppression is the Irish habit of answering questions with other questions rather than risk useful intelligence falling into the hands of the enemy. Thus, the correct response to the greeting "How're ya?" is to say "How're ya?" back. This is a perfectly polite exchange among Irish people since each knows that the other person's query was not serious. Or if it was, then he's a nosey bollocks, and you're not going to give him the satisfaction of a proper answer.

Outsiders will sometimes misinterpret the "How're ya?" greeting as an invitation to share their problems. This really is a mistake. The questioner will probably listen politely as you detail your recent medical history, or the progress you've made in therapy, but you sure as hell won't be asked a second time. Not only that, but word will get around, and soon people will cross the street when they see you coming.

Sense of Humour

Long the butt of English jokes portraying them as stupid, the Irish have traditionally been on the defensive when it comes to humour. They tried displacement, and having no small neighbours to the west picked on Kerry, the Irish county furthest from Dublin. But the vogue for jokes about how dumb Kerry people were died of shame.

They also tried retaliation, with gags that portrayed the English as wooden straight-men, mere foils for the Irishman's quick wit.

> **66 The Irish have traditionally been on the defensive when it comes to humour. 99**

One epic series revolves around the activities of an unlikely trio: Paddy the Irishman, Paddy the Englishman, and Paddy the Scotsman. In the best of these, the Irishman walks a fine line between naivete and cunning, as if to explain how anyone could ever have been stupid enough to think he was stupid:

Three Paddys are organising a church collection and wrestling with the idea of how much to give. Paddy the Englishman explains that he always draws a line on the ground. "I throw all the money up in the air. What falls to the left of the line, I keep and what falls to the right I give to the church."

Paddy the Scotsman explains that he prefers to

draw a circle on the ground. "I too throw the money up in the air. What falls outside the circle I keep, and what falls inside I give to the church."

Paddy the Irishman explains that he doesn't draw anything: "I just throw all the money up in the air. And what God doesn't want he throws down again."

But if truth be told, the Irishman's heart is not in these jokes, which are merely an exasperated response to centuries of cultural misunderstanding. The Scotsman in the Paddy jokes betrays this. He's only there to set up the Englishman, or occasionally as mere ballast in the narrative – an example of the story-tellers' rule of three. He is the neutral pin in the plug and the Englishman is the earth; or vice versa. The Irishman always gets to play the live-wire.

If there is an intrinsically Irish sense of humour, it resides in story-telling.

If there is an intrinsically Irish sense of humour, it resides in story-telling, which may be why Ireland has produced so many 'alternative' comedians. It is also inextricably bound up with the craic. Once the craic is invoked among a group, anything can happen, and the result is a great fondness for practical jokes, especially in rural areas.

Sadly, practical jokes are not as elaborate as they once were, thanks to a rise in litigation and a fall in the amount of time on people's hands. In pre-motorised Ireland, a notorious joke – practised on someone who had been drinking heavily and was sleeping it off – involved dismantling his donkey's cart and reassembling it inside his kitchen. The donkey would then be led in through the front door – he would just about fit – and re-harnessed to the cart. Some people may have given up drink as a result of this prank.

Culture

Traditional music

Traditional music is a cornerstone of Irish culture, and central to it is the 'session', in which a number of musicians get together to play tunes, typically in a pub. To the unsuspecting, this may seem like an informal arrangement. But don't be deceived. The apparently casual behaviour of session musicians is in fact as highly regulated as that of ants.

> **Traditional music is a cornerstone of Irish culture, and central to it is the 'session'.**

Don't be deceived either by the apparent inclusiveness of the group, which seems to welcome all newcomers and their instruments equally. The traditional session is a minefield of etiquette. If you are, for example, a guitar player, you might be advised to

45

tread carefully. In some sessions, you might even be advised to tread on the guitar.

The first rule of the session is that the music must be traditional. You're probably thinking that there must be a helpful definition somewhere explaining what exactly the word 'traditional' means. Ha ha! If only it were as simple as that. The Irish did not endure Eight Hundred Years of Oppression so that any damn tourist can arrive and pass himself off as one of them.

No. The understanding of what is or is not traditional has been passed on orally or telepathically, like the music itself, from generation to generation; but never in such a form that it could fall into the hands of the authorities. Experienced players can tell a non-traditional tune just from its rhythm and feel – or sometimes from its smell, if their senses are particularly developed. In fundamentalist strongholds such as Clare – the Mecca of traditional music – disputes on what is traditional may be referred to bearded holy men who ensure that the music is played in accordance with rules laid down in the 5th century.

> **❝ Experienced players can tell a non-traditional tune just from its rhythm and feel – or sometimes from its smell. ❞**

Traditional instruments include fiddle, tin whistle and flute. Non-traditional instruments include guitar, piano and Peruvian pan-pipes. However, thanks to globalism, the bouzouki and bodhran (a one-sided drum made from goat skin) are now often seen in sessions and tolerated (at least publicly). Musicians may express their disapproval in subtle ways, such as by getting up and leaving.

Singing is acceptable at a session provided it is of the traditional variety known as 'Sean Nós' (pronounced 'Shan Noce'). This usually means that the song should

> **66** Audiences are not crucial to the session which in small pubs can take up the entire premises anyway, leaving no room for listeners. **99**

tell a story and preferably be in Irish. It should also either (a) have 36 verses or (b) go on all night – whichever is longer.

Ballad singing is frowned upon, and group sing-songs will usually result in ejection from the premises. However long they take, Sean Nós songs must be heard in rapt silence, except during the pauses between verses, when listeners may shout encouragement in the manner of worshippers in a Mississippi Baptist church. But audiences are not crucial to the session which in small pubs can take up the entire premises anyway, leaving no room for listeners. The musicians are essentially playing for each other.

Irish dancing

There are two main kinds of Irish dancing: (1) Riverdance, the stage spectacular at one time running in more cities in the world than tap water; and (2) Real Irish Dancing. The latter has many similarities to Riverdance but exists mainly in competitive form. Other differences are that, in Real Irish Dancing, men do not wear frilly blouses and dancers may not express themselves (except in a written note to the adjudicators).

Until 1994 there was only Real Irish Dancing. Unlike most national dance forms, such as flamenco or tango, it had no sexual undertone of any sort. All traces of sensuality had been carefully removed by the combined effects of competition and the strict Catholic upbringing to which most dancers were sub-jected. Arms were held rigidly by the sides, as if glued there. Backs were even more rigid. Excessive hip movement could be punished by loss of marks or – in extreme cases – excommunication from the church.

> **❝Real Irish dancing had no sexual undertone of any sort. Excessive hip movement could be punished by loss of marks.❞**

Then along came Michael Flatley, a multiple World Irish Dancing Champion from Chicago. Bored with convention, Flatley introduced a freer style of Irish dance, one that exuded sexuality. Key to his approach was the idea that the arms need not be held rigid. Instead, dancers could – gasp – wave them around. Like Greeks!

Riverdance, with Flatley in the lead male role,

began life as an interval act during the 1994 Eurovision song contest in Dublin. The sight of Irish dancers moving their arms freely and swivelling their hips had a cathartic effect on the audience. It was as if Ireland threw off centuries of repression, there and then. It may be no coincidence that 1994 also saw peace in Northern Ireland and the start of the Republic's economic boom.

> **66 The sight of Irish dancers moving their arms freely and swivelling their hips had a cathartic effect. 99**

Meanwhile Real Irish Dancing continues pretty much as before. But its long-repressed sexuality is now smouldering, and competition organisers have fire marshals at all venues, just in case.

Literature

Irish writers

Writers occupy a powerful position in Irish society: the wall of the local pub, to be exact. Walk into a typical Dublin bar, and you'll see their pictures: Joyce and Beckett, Yeats and Wilde, Shaw, O'Casey, O'Brien and Behan, watching over you as you drink, like secular saints. The prominence given to them does not imply that the bar owner has actually read their books. In fact, for some cynical publicans, the writers are merely providing posthumous product endorsement. Many of them liked a drink and became literary geniuses: bar flies are invited to draw their own conclusions.

But the connection between literature and pubs may run deeper than that. To understand the importance of Irish writers, you have to understand Ireland's ancient bardic tradition. Bards were highly esteemed. They were at least on a par with cattle in the eyes of the country's feudal leaders, who craved their praise and feared their curses equally. Chieftains who treated bards with less than the respect they demanded did so at their peril. In short, the bardic tradition was a literary protection racket.

> **66 Bards were highly esteemed. They were at least on a par with cattle in the eyes of the country's feudal leaders. 99**

Looked at in this light, publicans who invoke the great Irish writers may be subconsciously taking out insurance. If some up-and-coming literary punk tries to lean on them (for, say, free drink) they can point to the wall and say: "Sorry, I'm already paying off those guys."

Thanks to a modern chieftain, Irish writers enjoy tax-free status. A former prime minister, Charles J. Haughey, was an enthusiastic patron of the arts. In introducing the tax exemption he may have hoped, like the chieftains of old, for a sympathetic portrayal. If so, his big mistake was not including journalists in the scheme. His wealth has been the subject of a series of exposés and his retirement dogged by scandals – including, ironically, his underpayment of tax.

The urge to write

For a nation that talks a lot, the Irish produce an extraordinary amount of literature. In fact, only the tendency to talk too much keeps the literary surplus at controllable levels.

Literary genius is common – there are four Nobel prizes to show for it – and critics suggest it's only talent that is scarce. At any rate, it is said that every Irish person has a book inside him or her. Very few can be persuaded to leave it there.

> **❝It is said that every Irish person has a book inside him or her. Very few can be persuaded to leave it there.❞**

Many reasons have been advanced for the Irish literary phenomenon. No doubt a part of it is that Irish people are good at writing because they're good at talking. After all, in a country where there are so few listeners, people get used to talking to themselves, and from there it's only a short step to writing.

The Irish language must be a factor, adding under-soil heating to the sometimes-frozen pitch surface of English. Even writers who don't speak it draw on the rhythms and idioms of Irish, whether they want to or not. But turbulent history is a proven inspiration to art, and with Eight Hundred Years of Oppression in the bank, Irish writers can live off the interest. Even the local weather – the low skies, the rain, and the grey light – is offered as an explanation for the urge to write. It's claimed that these conditions inspire intro-spection, flights of fancy, and a kind of madness that, if channelled, can produce literature.

Some have argued for a link between poverty and creativity. The Irish have had a deep reservoir of misery to draw on, and it inspired a number of major books including the mega-selling,

> **" The low skies, the rain, and the grey light – is offered as an explanation for the urge to write. "**

Angela's Ashes. But if poverty and oppression are an inspiration to literature, it goes without saying that the current peace and prosperity present Irish writers with their biggest ever challenge.

Food

To the despair of gourmets, the definitive Irish meal is the fried breakfast. And reflecting the political divi-sions on the island, this comes in two forms: the 'Full Irish', which is served throughout the Republic and in Catholic areas of the North; and the 'Ulster Fry', which is generally confined to the Protestant north-east.

Both contain bacon, eggs, sausages, and black and white pudding (made from parts of animals you'd rather not think about). Liver and kidneys may be thrown in, when available. Fried potato cakes and fried bread are optional.

> **" As with many differences that the Irish consider defining, it may be difficult for outsiders to tell the breakfasts apart. "**

As with many differences that the Irish consider defining, it may be difficult for outsiders to tell the breakfasts apart. The truth is, nobody in Ireland knows the difference between them either. There's a suspicion that the Ulster Fry may have 10% extra cholesterol, in keeping with the Protestant work ethic. But if you eat enough of them, they'll both kill you in the long run.

Sport

Gaelic games

No-one who wants to understand the Irish can do so without first understanding the Gaelic Athletic Association. Founded in 1884 to revive Gaelic games, and to promote Irish culture generally, the GAA is now the envy of all other sporting organisations on the island. It has clubs in every town and hamlet, and wields the sort of influence over Irish life that the government can only hope to achieve, one day.

The GAA's two main games are football and hurling. Gaelic football combines elements of soccer (a round ball, goalkeepers) with elements of rugby (hand-passing, organised violence). Violence is a part of hurling too, with the crucial difference that –

> **66 No matter how high the fans' passions run, once the final whistle goes, all animosity is quickly forgotten. 99**

thanks to the hockey-style sticks involved – fights are armed. Also the ball in hurling spends much of its time in the air – around head-height. Because of this, many players wear helmets. But many do not, either because of old-fashioned machismo, or because they're just tired of having full sets of teeth.

A proud boast of the movement is that any bad feeling stays on the pitch. Opposing GAA fans are never segregated, no matter how great their rivalry. And no matter how high the fans' passions run, once the final whistle goes, all animosity is quickly forgotten. Incidents in which the match referee is assaulted and locked in the boot of his own car – while not unknown – are rare.

The crowning glory of the GAA is that its players are not paid, even though they attract crowds of up to 80,000 people to the big matches. The reward for a player who makes it big in the sport is often to open a pub. Many GAA players also go on to success in local and national politics just as surely as army generals do in Africa, but usually without the need for a coup.

The big drawback of Gaelic sport is that it has no real international outlet. Hurling and Gaelic football are played among the diaspora in Britain and America. But marketing the sports to a broader constituency is a problem, especially in the U.S. where 'hurling' is something you do when you have a violent stomach upset.

Horses for courses

Never mind Gaelic football and hurling, Ireland's real national sport is horse-racing. It has been said that Ireland is to horse-racing what Brazil is to soccer. And if you think this is a slight exaggeration, you're probably right. The Brazilians are not that good.

> **It has been said that Ireland is to horse-racing what Brazil is to soccer.**

Equestrianism is big business in Ireland. The breeding, training, and racing of horses directly employs up to 25,000 people, and supports numerous ancillary industries, of which hat manufacture is a small example. Horse owners and trainers are the only people in Ireland who wear hats, and without them, the millinery sector would collapse overnight.

The heartland of Irish racing is the Curragh, a limestone plain in County Kildare famous for its short but calcium-rich grass. The plains of Kildare have bred countless champions. Crucially for Irish racing, they also bred the Finance Minister who preserved tax-free status for stallions' stud fees. Such enthusiasm for horses is not unusual among Irish politicians. If the government had to hold an emergency Cabinet meeting during mid-March, its best chance of finding a quorum would be in England in the parade ring at Cheltenham, where the Gold Cup meeting is an annual pilgrimage for thousands of Irish horse-worshippers.

> **If the government had to hold an emergency Cabinet meeting in March, its best chance of finding a quorum would be in the parade ring at Cheltenham.**

The Irish grip on jumps racing, in particular, is such that some of the top 'English' trainers are Irish. And if they could speak, many English horses, like Denman, would do so in faint Irish accents, remembered from their childhoods in Kildare and such places.

> **If they could speak, many English horses would do so in faint Irish accents.**

A majority of the top jockeys in Britain are also Irish. Ireland operates a conveyor belt of these small but fearless people that few countries can match. And whereas all the best Brazilian football players now end up in Europe, the strength of Irish horse racing is such that some of the best jockeys stay at home.

Obsession

The weather

Ireland has an extraordinary amount of weather for a small country. By far the highest concentrations occur along the western sea-board. But smaller deposits are distributed all across the country; even in Wexford and Waterford – the part of Ireland humorously known as the 'sunny south-east'.

Much of the weather originates hundreds of miles out to sea in the form of so-called 'Atlantic weather systems'. By the time it reaches Ireland, however, any trace of a system has usually disappeared. In Kerry, as you'd find out when trying to plan a picnic, it's not unusual to experience all four seasons in the same afternoon.

> **The temperature of the rain is often the only reliable clue to what time of year it is.**

The Irish talk about the weather constantly which results in a certain amount of exaggeration. Ireland's weather is not nearly as interesting as the Irish pretend. There are no real extremes. Winters are mild, summers are cool, and the temperature of the rain is often the only reliable clue to what time of year it is.

The tendency to dramatise the climate does not extend to preparing for it. In fact, with the contrariness of which Freud despaired, the Irish manage simultaneously to exaggerate the weather while being in denial about it. Despite overwhelming evidence that it rains a lot, few people own proper waterproof clothes. Possession of a good umbrella marks you out as fussy. Many Irish secretly scoff at visitors who tour Ireland in tent-sized raincoats, as if *they* are the eccentrics.

> **"After as few as two consecutive dry days, they react with shock to the return of rain as a betrayal by the elements. "**

Deep down the Irish believe that a century of recorded weather statistics is just a run of bad luck that's bound to end soon. Thus, after as few as two consecutive dry days, they react with shock to the return of rain as a betrayal by the elements that could not have been foreseen. It's one of the great paradoxes of the Irish: the inclination to talk about the weather all the time and never to learn anything from the conversation.

Attitudes & Values

The licensing laws

Few things illustrate the contrariness of the Irish as well as their contrasting attitudes towards drink and tobacco. When Ireland became the first country in Europe to ban smoking in pubs and restaurants, many experts predicted the law was doomed to fail, with even the government minister responsible admitting it might need a 'bedding-in period'.

Instead, the Irish embraced the ban with something like the enthusiasm of born-again Christians embracing Jesus. Non-smokers welcomed the clear air in pubs. Smokers welcomed the impetus to give up a bad habit. Contrary to the pessimists' hastily revised opinions, not even winter killed off the ban.

> **"The search for after-hours drink remains a holy grail for many alcohol enthusiasts. "**

The contrast with Ireland's drink laws would be sobering – if that were not the wrong word. Although many of these laws are more than 100 years old, the bedding-in period continues.

The search for after-hours drink remains a holy grail for many alcohol enthusiasts, and still confers a real sense of achievement on those who find it. Even the most refined palates agree that no beer tastes as good as the one drunk after official closing time. And although the opportunities have grown fewer, this only adds to the prize for those who successfully defy the licensing laws.

Make mine a double standard

Because most of the licensing laws date from British times, they are sometimes seen as a legacy of the Eight Hundred Years of Oppression. In this light, after-hours drinking is an act of quiet patriotism.

When a newspaper reported that the Minister for Finance had celebrated his budget with an after-hours 'lock-in' (when the pub is only closed from the outside), it was the story that was demoted – to the outer fringes of public interest. Many people wondered what the world was coming to, that a newspaper didn't have something better to be writing about.

> **66 The traditional afternoon closing of pubs used to be known as the 'Holy Hour', after a church observance. 99**

There are explanations for this double standard. Defiance of the church may once have been a factor too. The traditional afternoon closing of pubs used to be known as the 'Holy Hour', after a church observance popular with Catholics. Drinkers who managed to avoid leaving a pub during the afternoon closing were said to be 'doing the Holy Hour' (although this was never a defence accepted by the courts).

The dichotomy has given rise to some bizarre situations in the wake of the smoking ban. Don't be surprised, for instance, if in some remote Irish pubs you see customers interrupting their illegal after-hours drinking at regular intervals to go outside to smoke – in accordance with the law.

The demon drink

In America, the term 'pioneers' refers to those intrepid migrants who gradually pushed back the frontiers of the United States and eventually tamed a continent. In Ireland, 'the Pioneers' are a movement set up in the 1890s to curb the nation's drinking. This tells you all you need to know about Ireland's epic struggle with alcohol.

> **A home-made fire-water, poteen did to many Irish drinkers what the Apaches did to white settlers.**

The Irish Pioneer movement did not get its name by accident. Its founder, a Catholic priest, was inspired by stories of fearless New World settlers battling hostile terrain, disease, severe winters, and fierce bands of Indians as they trekked westward in their painted wagons, searching for free land and a better life. Obviously he thought that imposing temperance on the Irish would be a similar challenge.

The U.S. and Ireland of his time had something in common: a wild west. The early Irish Pioneers had the benefit of Victorian licensing laws in the east, with concepts such as closing time. But outside Dublin, the grip of the law eased. West of the river Shannon – Ireland's Mississippi – was an untamed wilderness populated by shebeen keepers (unlicensed publicans) and poteen makers. A home-made fire-water, poteen did to many Irish drinkers what the Apaches did to white settlers.

The problem was exacerbated by the fact that whiskey was a cheap option for the impoverished masses. Ale was a luxury by comparison.

The Pioneers were and remain an elite group, and are not to be confused with Alcoholics Anonymous. The movement's founders despaired of converting hard drinkers, so the Pioneers' emphasis was on organising the teetotal minority to provide a public example to the less virtuous. Members still 'take the pledge' by promising to remain sober, and are given small badges to wear on their lapels, like war heroes.

> **" Members still 'take the pledge' and are given small badges to wear on their lapels, like war heroes. "**

Shebeens are long gone, poteen is nearly extinct, and the licensing laws have spread to all corners of Ireland. But the battle is far from won. On the contrary, the economic boom has removed one of Ireland's traditional restraints against drinking – lack of money. The Irish continue to suffer high levels of alcoholism: a fact all the more striking because the nation also has unusually high levels of total abstinence. One in four Irish people never touch a drink, which makes the statistical achievements of the rest of them all the more impressive.

> **" The economic boom has removed one of Ireland's traditional restraints against drinking – lack of money. "**

Religion

Until only a few years ago, the Republic of Ireland was the most devoutly religious country in Europe, overwhelmingly Roman Catholic and proud of it.

But while the faith may have thrived on persecution and poverty, it was to face a more insidious enemy in the form of economic success.

By the mid-1990s there was peace in Northern Ireland, but in the Republic the struggle between God and Mammon was spilling over into full-scale war. The conflict rages even now, with Mammon claiming control of large parts of the urbanised east, while God's influence is confined to the poorer areas of the border, midlands, and west (or 'the BMW region'). But soul-searching has become a popular pastime among the Irish everywhere, so all may not be lost for religion yet.

> **❝Death is a very public event in Ireland, a country where people are never so popular as just after they've stopped breathing.❞**

The decline in spirituality can be overstated. The trappings of Catholicism are still very much apparent, such as people crossing themselves when they pass a church, or the fact that the state television broadcasts the Angelus bells – a call to prayer – at noon and 6 p.m. daily. However, the visuals accompanying the Angelus have been toned down to make it more acceptable to non-Catholics. They now just feature a range of people pausing in their everyday activities and, instead of crossing themselves, staring reflectively into the distance. It's like a quieter version of a National Lottery ad.

Church attendance is still high by European standards, but it has fallen dramatically, as has the political influence of the pulpit. The rise in materialism coincided with a series of sex scandals that badly undermined the church's authority, and religious vocations have plummeted. Ireland used to produce so many priests that there was always a big surplus available for export to missions in Africa and elsewhere. Irish priests are still very much involved with charities in the developing world, but it's a sign of the shift in power that, these days, Ireland's highest-profile missionaries to Africa are Bob Geldof and Bono.

❝It's a sign of the shift in power that, these days, Ireland's highest-profile missionaries to Africa are Bob Geldof and Bono.❞

Catholics are the majority denomination in both parts of Ireland: about 90% in the Republic, where the biggest minority religion is known – confusingly – as the Church of Ireland. The C of I is part of the world-wide Anglican community, and is one of the churches that help make Northern Ireland predominantly Protestant. The Presbyterians are the largest of these churches, the breakaway Free Presbyterians being the best known thanks to their very noisy founder, Reverend Ian Paisley.

The Irish mother

The Irish Mother – usually known to her offspring as 'Mammy' – does not wield quite as much influence as she did in the days when she had 10 or 11 children working for her cause. Now she often has to hold down a job outside the home as well, devolving some of her power to child-minders. But her role is still exalted by centuries-old tradition, and she has so far escaped the sort of criticism visited on the other pillars of Irish life, like the church and the GAA.

> **Unlike the many martyrs who died for Ireland, the Irish mother is the martyr who lives for it.**

Unlike the many martyrs who died for Ireland, the Irish mother is the martyr who lives for it. Her heroic self-sacrifice is celebrated in umpteen songs, of which the old-time waltz *A Mother's Love is a Blessing* is a classic example. Sung by an emigrating son, its chorus – simultaneously jaunty and guilt-crippled – ends with the line 'You'll never miss your mother's love/Till she's buried beneath the clay'. And this sentiment touches upon a key concept of the Irish mother: that despite the evidence of songs like this one, her sacrifice is unappreciated.

This idea has launched a number of cruel jokes, e.g:

Q: "How many Irish mothers does it take to change a light-bulb?"

A: "None. Sure amn't I grand sitting here in the dark?"

These jokes are particularly popular with women. For while the Irish Mother aspires to cherish all her children equally, many daughters allege her bias in favour of sons. Indeed, it tends to be the Irish son who puts his mother on a pedestal (albeit one where she has plenty of room to wash and cook for him).

> **❝ It tends to be the Irish son who puts his mother on a pedestal (albeit one where she has plenty of room to wash and cook for him). ❞**

Another feminist joke argues that Jesus Christ must have been Irish because he lived at home until he was 30, he thought his mother was a virgin, and she thought he was the son of God.

But a strange thing happens to many feminists when they themselves have children. The powerful Irish Mother gene – until then dormant – suddenly seizes control of their bodies, and alters their personalities irrevocably. Thus the DNA is successfully passed on to another generation of women. Before they know it, they have turned into

> **❝ The powerful Irish Mother gene seizes control of their bodies, and alters their personalities irrevocably. ❞**

Mammies, super-sizing portions by going short themselves, and promoting their cooking with such catchy slogans as "Get that into you, son, it'll do you good".

Death

Irish people have a favourite euphemism for death. The standard expression of sympathy at a funeral, delivered while shaking hands with the bereaved, is: "I'm sorry for your troubles." This is said whether the deceased has died of natural causes aged 103, or was the victim of a drive-by shooting in a drugs feud. But its popularity does not imply that death is a taboo subject.

> **Death is a very public event in Ireland, a country where people are never so popular as just after they've stopped breathing.**

Far from it. Death is a very public event in Ireland, a country where people are never so popular as just after they've stopped breathing. Obituary pages are among the most avidly read in Irish newspapers, and local radio stations routinely broadcast the death notices for their areas, reading them out like a slightly more solemn version of the football results.

Well into the 20th century, the three-day wake was common throughout Ireland. In many respects this resembled what in other cultures would be called a party, involving as it did large-scale indulgence in alcohol, tobacco, and snuff. And while there was a spiritual basis to the wake – it was essentially a diversionary tactic, to throw evil spirits off the trail while the soul of the deceased made a safe getaway to the next world – the church was always a bit nervous about the custom.

The old-style wake is gone now, and the celebratory element of Irish funerals has waned somewhat. When people were poor and religious, departure to the next world was an attractive option, which was why many sick people sent for a priest (to ensure there'd be no problems at the frontier) rather than a doctor. Nowadays, the lure of the next world is not what it used to be, and doctors are more in demand.

> **66 For many Irish people serial funeral attendance is a pastime. 99**

But if the celebratory aspect of the Irish funeral has declined, it remains an important social outlet. For many Irish people serial funeral attendance is a pastime. In fact, if you're a politician, attending as many of them as possible – if only long enough to shake hands with the bereaved and say "Sorry for your troubles" – remains absolutely crucial to your prospects of being re-elected.

Belief in the supernatural

The human Irish share space with a wide assortment of supernatural beings, known collectively as 'the fairies'. By far the best known of these are the Leprechauns, a diminutive race of expert shoemakers. But their fame has less to do with shoe-making than with their secondary role as guardians of ancient treasure, to which humans who catch them may be led.

Although very industrious, leprechauns are notorious for drinking poteen. This can make them careless, and more liable to be seen. By a curious coincidence, many of the reported sightings of leprechauns have been by humans who had been drinking poteen too. Suffice to say, the treasure remains unclaimed.

The Irish do not distinguish between good and evil fairies. Although fond of mischief, Irish fairies are never bad, just misunderstood. But the most feared

> **❝ By a curious coincidence, many of the reported sightings of leprechauns have been by humans who had been drinking too. ❞**

of them is the Pooka, a night-walking spirit, the mere sight of whom is said to stop hens from laying. The Pooka can take many forms – from a wild horse to a goat, from a giant eagle to a big, hairy bogeyman – and it has been known to throw people it meets into drains or bogholes. Again, those who've been drinking poteen are especially vulnerable.

Just as feared, but for very different reasons, is the Banshee whose wail has been described as anything from low singing to a sound so piercing it can shatter glass. Her famous cry warns members of five Irish families – the O'Briens, the O'Connors, the O'Gradys, the O'Neills, and the Kavanaghs – of impending death. But thanks to intermarriage down the centuries, many Irish people without those surnames are liable to hear the Banshee.

The Banshee may be seen too, sometimes in the form of a washer-woman laundering the blood-stained clothes of those about to die. But in common with Pookas, leprechauns, and other spirits, her appearances seem to have become much rarer since the electrification of rural Ireland in the 1950s. Light pollution is generally blamed for the decline.

Customs

St. Patrick's Day

No matter where you are in the world, with one exception, 17th March has always been a great day to be Irish. The exception is Ireland itself, where until recently St. Patrick's Day was regarded with scepticism.

66 Those for whom being Irish was a full-time job didn't quite see the point in celebrating. 99

From Liverpool to New York, from Toronto to Melbourne, it was an occasion of ethnic pride, when even tenth generation emigrants celebrated their Irishness by wearing green, dyeing the local rivers green, and even drinking green beer. Meanwhile, back at headquarters, the inhabitants of the sainted isle itself tended to wear anything except green, and struggled to muster any enthusiasm for the event.

It was a national holiday, and you didn't have to go to work. But for many people it was a day of rest rather than celebration. It was all right for Irish-Americans to let their hair down once a year. Those for whom being Irish was a full-time job didn't quite see the point in celebrating. It was as if the burden of responsibility weighed them down. The fact that mid-March in Ireland is almost guaranteed to produce some of the year's most vicious weather didn't help.

66 The suspicion lingers that the whole Paddy's Day thing has been foisted on them by the Americans. 99

Patrick's Day parades were being held by the Irish abroad for a century before it occurred to the Irish at home to do likewise, and even then the Dublin version was half-hearted. But around the same time as Riverdance, the Dublin parade was transformed into a big production – a sort of cold-weather Mardi Gras.

The national holiday is not just a 24-hour event anymore: it's a five-day festival with everything from fireworks displays to symposiums, in which intellectuals discuss the meaning of being Irish. Of the old-style Paddy's Day, only the weather remains.

Attendance at the Dublin parade still does not include the government, however. The importance of the diaspora means that in mid-March almost every minister will be overseas – attending Irish parties.

Back at home, Irish people celebrate with a bit more enthusiasm than they used to. But the suspicion lingers that the whole Paddy's Day thing has been foisted on them by the Americans. And they still draw the line at green beer.

Halloween

Halloween is in some respects the opposite of St. Patrick's Day. Where the Irish have been slow to embrace the latter – a Christian festival – they have been revelling in the former – a pagan one – for going on 2,000 years. And whereas the Irish have overcome their queasiness about St. Patrick's Day to reclaim it from the Americans, the Americans have overcome their queasiness about Halloween, stolen it outright from the Irish and Scots, and are now trying to sell it back to them, and to the rest of the world, at a mark-up.

66 Many of the customs still practised in Ireland started out as attempts to keep evil spirits in check, or to manipulate their presence in the interests of the living. 99

The repackaging of Halloween as an autumn consumer festival is remarkable for an event that began as nothing less than a Day of the Living Dead. To the ancient Celts, 1st November was the turning of the year, and the night before was a time when the borders between the temporal and spirit worlds blurred. Many of the customs still practised in Ireland started out as attempts to keep evil spirits in check, or to manipulate their presence in the interests of the living.

When the Irish light bonfires on 31st October, they mimic the huge fires once lit by druids to invite the waning sun to return in spring (something the Celts never took for granted). When Irish children go door-to-door saying 'trick or treat', they practise a form of blackmail that probably originated when farmers left out food for hungry spirits so that cattle and crops would not be damaged.

> **"The idea of evil spirits running amok on 31st October survives."**

The nearness of the spirits meant that all sorts of secrets could be divined on Halloween Night. Young couples roasted nuts on a fire, for example, to foretell their marital prospects. If the nuts nestled together in the embers, they would get on well. If the nuts jumped apart, pre-marriage counselling might be in order.

Those beliefs have died out, but the idea of evil spirits running amok on 31st October survives, albeit that the work of the spirits is now usually carried out by young boys and men. A typical Halloween prank used to be to cover someone's chimney, thereby filling the house with smoke. Nowadays it's more often innocent stuff such as ringing doorbells and running away.

One shade of orange

While the colour green has long been synonymous with Irish nationalism, the other theme in Ireland's history – pro-British unionism – is represented by orange. This symbolises King William of Orange, whose victory at the Battle of Boyne in 1690 ensured the Protestant ascendancy in Ireland for two centuries.

The Orange Order continues to celebrate the battle every 12th July. This is the highlight of Northern Ireland's so-called 'marching season' which runs from about the start of May each year to the end of the following April. Long before the modern craze for aerobic exercise, Orangemen were keeping themselves fit by power-walking all over the north. But fitness was not the main motivation.

> **Ireland's so-called 'marching season' runs from about the start of May each year to the end of the following April.**

Indeed, the exercise value of the chosen routes has sometimes been added to by the need to dodge bricks and petrol bombs thrown by Catholics. The triumphalist nature of some marches and the fact that they often passed through nationalist areas made them very contentious. Eventually a parades commission was formed to rule on disputed routes, and these days most flash-points are avoided.

The modern Irish tricolour is a graphic attempt to combine the traditions of green and orange with the white of peace between them. But memories die hard in Ireland and the Battle of the Boyne is still a bit too recent for everybody involved to bury the hatchet.

Green and orange musical instruments

Ireland is the only country in the world whose official symbol is a musical instrument. The harp spans both political traditions on the island, appearing on all state documents in the Republic, while also representing Ireland on the British royal standard. This is unusual, because in Ireland, not even musical instruments are allowed to be politically neutral.

The fiddle, for example, represents the Catholic-nationalist-republican tradition, whereas the flute, because of its long association with northern loyalist flute bands, is seen as a Protestant-unionist instrument.

> **"In Ireland, not even musical instruments are allowed to be politically neutral."**

The North's musical traditions are illustrated by an old joke about an education inspector who visits a school in the Catholic Sperrin mountains. Testing the children's vocabulary, he asks them: "What do you call a piano player?" A hand shoots up with the answer: "A pianist, sir." And so it goes until the inspector asks the word for a flute player. Silence descends on the class, until the inspector probes: "Come, come. Surely, somebody can tell me what you call a flute player."

Finally a shy hand creeps up. "Yes?" says the inspector. "Sir, at home we call him an orange bastard."

Government

Few nations have embraced the concept of representative democracy with quite the enthusiasm of the Irish. For example, the Republic's four million people elect 166 members of parliament, a ratio of 24,000 to 1. If this model were followed elsewhere, Britain's House of Commons would have 2,500 members, and the parliament of India would have to meet in a football stadium.

> **❝Few nations have embraced the concept of representative democracy with quite the enthusiasm of the Irish. ❞**

Add the fact that Northern Ireland has a 108-member regional assembly while continuing to send 18 Members of Parliament to Westminster, and you can see why some people on the island think an annual cull of politicians is needed to keep the numbers down to sustainable levels.

The *Dail*

The Republic's parliament is called the *Dail* (pronounced 'Dhoil'), and its members (TDs) are elected by proportional representation, based on the single transferable vote in multiple-seat constituencies.

The main advantage of this system is fairness: a party that wins 40% of the vote will generally win 40% of the seats. Another big advantage – now threatened by electronic voting – is that election counts can go on for several days, providing the public with cheap entertainment at the expense of nervous politicians whose futures depend on picking up a handful of lower-preference votes in the 17th count. The big downside of multiple-seat constituencies is that, instead of just vying with opposition parties, candidates more often have to defend their backs against dagger-wielding colleagues. But this can be entertaining too.

> **66 Election counts can go on for several days, providing the public with cheap entertainment. 99**

The dominant party in the Republic is *Fianna Fail* – meaning 'Soldiers of Destiny' – a populist movement of the centre-left or centre-right (depending on wind conditions). Like the second-biggest party, *Fine Gael*, 'Family of the Gael', *Fianna Fail* grew out of the Civil War of 1922-3. *Fine Gael* won that war, but they haven't won much since. In fact, from the 1930s onwards, only *Fianna Fail* has ever secured an overall majority in a general election. Partly because of the Civil War – in which the Labour Party abstained – Ireland never developed the traditional left-right divide. So while *Fine Gael* is apparently forever condemned to second place, Labour has always finished third.

Proportional representation makes it hard for any party to win a majority, however, so most modern governments are formed by coalitions. This suits the Irish electorate very well. Instinctively conservative but suspicious of ideology, voters choose governments in the same way that they would mix paint. *Fianna Fail* is usually the base colour, to which the electorate adds a dash of red (Labour) or blue (the tax-cutting Progressive Democrats), according to mood. Occasionally, voters go mad altogether and choose a Rainbow Coalition, around *Fine Gael*.

> **66 Instinctively conservative but suspicious of ideology, Irish voters choose governments in the same way that they would mix paint. 99**

The colour range has been extended in recent years with the emergence of the Greens and the militant nationalists *Sinn Fein* (meaning 'We Ourselves') as *Dail* parties. *Sinn Fein* is unique in that it fights elections in both the North and the South. It's also unique in having an armed wing, the IRA (Irish Republican Army, known to supporters simply as 'the Army').

Since the Irish state also has an organisation called The Army, there would a potential conflict of interest should *Sinn Fein* ever feature in a coalition government. This is a vexed issue, which only the disbandment of the IRA would solve. The normally

pro-enterprise Progressive Democrats have been particularly vociferous in suggesting that the defence of
the state is one area where consumers would not benefit from increased competition.

The *Seanad*

Unlike Britain, Ireland has neither an aristocracy nor a
state honours system. The nearest thing to hereditary
peers are people whose grandfathers were in or near
Dublin's General Post Office
in 1916 when it was the
headquarters for the Easter
Rising against British rule.
Political dynasties – many of
them rising phoenix-like from

> **"The nearest thing to
> hereditary peers are people
> whose grandfathers were in
> or near Dublin's General
> Post Office in 1916."**

the ashes of the GPO – are a familiar feature of Irish
politics, although no matter how good your pedigree
in Ireland, at some stage you will usually have to
suffer the indignity of standing for election.

The Irish equivalent of the House of Lords is the
Seanad, or Senate, which is elected by a number of
panels representing different interests, including the
universities. It was formed partly as a forum for the
south's minority Protestant population, but also to
ensure a voice for poets, intellectuals, eccentrics, etc.,
who might not be heard in the 'lower' house. Indeed,
one of the early senators was W. B. Yeats who fell into

all these categories.

In more recent times, the Senate has been criticised as an irrelevant talking shop. But it has played a vital supporting role in Ireland's democracy, providing a kind of welfare system for politicians who have fallen on hard times. Senate elections follow general elections, and are therefore a safety net for those rejected by the electorate at large. The incoming government also has 11 Senate seats in its gift, and these are the basis of a benevolent fund aimed at keeping politicians viable until the next general election.

> **" Senate elections follow general elections, and are therefore a safety net for those rejected by the electorate at large. "**

Places on the Senate's 'back to work' scheme are always in high demand, however. Former TDs are not normally allowed to remain in the Senate indefinitely. Should the applicant's appeal fail at a second or third general election, he will usually find himself forced to undergo retraining, before being gently eased back into civilian life.

Business

When the Irish embraced capitalism they embraced it with the enthusiasm they used to have for the church: hence companies like Ryanair, whose brash chief executive Michael O'Leary now owns 51% of Ireland's known reserves of self-confidence.

It used to be the case – or so it seemed – that the Irish were not that interested in money. The feeling was entirely mutual. Money, at least in the form of foreign investment, wasn't that interested in them either. Agricultural and underdeveloped, Ireland used to have a perennial unemployment problem, which was only kept under control by mass emigration. The 1980s were a bad time in many countries but, in 1987, if Ireland had been a house, the banks would have possessed it.

Then everything changed. Around 1990, Ireland caught the wave of a global upturn. The term 'Celtic Tiger' was heard for the first time, a mutant form of the Asian Tiger already transforming economies in that region. Unemployment fell to nothing. Emigration stopped. For the first time, immigrants started arriving, to fill the job vacancies.

The Irish are now workaholics, and nobody is more surprised than them. With a huge deficit of infrastructure like roads, but at last the money to redress it, the country is a building site, adding to the traffic jams that have become a feature of everyday life. More and more Irish people can afford cars, and they spend half the day in

> **The Irish are now workaholics, and nobody is more surprised than them.**

them, going to and from work. Luckily, the mobile phone was invented alongside the boom, or the country would have ground to a halt under the weight of success.

The debate about general Irish economic policy often boils down to a choice between American free-market economics and the European Union's social model, with high taxes and high levels of public service. Boston versus Berlin, in short. In practice, Boston is winning the argument hands down. Berlin may have paid for Ireland's new roads through EU funds. It may even have made the BMWs that clog them. But the cars are more likely to have been paid for by jobs in American high-tech companies, many of which – from Yahoo! to Google – now have their European headquarters in Ireland. And it doesn't hurt from an American point of view that the Irish speak English.

Systems

Education

The Irish education system is predominantly 'voluntary'. Sadly for feckless students, this does not mean they have a choice about whether to participate in it or not. It just means that most of the schools they go

to are owned or managed by private institutions –
usually religious orders. Most of the funding is provided by the state.

Education is compulso-
ry from the ages of six to
15. In practice, Irish children start school in the
September after their

> **Secondary school is divided into a three-year Junior cycle, which is compulsory; and a two or three-year Senior cycle which is not.**

fourth birthday. This could be a reflection of the
nation's innate hunger for learning, often denied to
them during the Eight Hundred Years of Oppression.
More likely, it reflects the almost total absence of pre-
school education in Ireland, and the fact that private
childcare costs an absolute fortune.

Children attend primary school from the age of
four until about 12, whereupon they graduate to sec-
ond-level. Secondary school is then divided into a
three-year Junior cycle, which is compulsory; and a
two or three-year Senior cycle culminating in the
Leaving Certificate examination, which is not. The
Leaving Cert sounds like something you do before you
emigrate; and sure enough, that was the reality for
generations of Irish people. But it got its name from
the fact that it used to mark the student's departure
from the education system to the workplace. Now at
least half of Irish students proceed to university or
other third-level colleges.

Irish is a compulsory subject at primary and secondary level, barring special exemptions. Once a prerequisite for many government jobs, the teaching of the language used to be done on a carrot-and-stick basis. The carrot was the 10% bonus you got for doing state exams using Irish; while the stick was an actual stick, used by teachers for beating the subject into you. In these more enlightened times, one of the big recent developments in education is the *Gaelscoil* movement, which aims to revive the language through total immersion.

Law and order

The Irish are not a law-abiding people. They're not exactly anarchists either. But they regard things like traffic lights, speed limits, and one-way-street signs as having an advisory role, rather than anything more binding, in the regulation of their affairs. The sale of fireworks, for example, is illegal in the Republic of Ireland. But for several weeks before Halloween every year, the night sky of Dublin resembles Beirut circa 1978.

66 They regard things like traffic lights, speed limits, and one-way-street signs as having an advisory role. 99

Because of the Eight Hundred Years of Oppression, many Irish people have an ambivalent attitude to the law. When somebody tells them they can't do something – such as have a drink in a pub after closing time – they immediately feel oppressed and want to fight against the injustice. So if you enter a pub in rural Ireland after midnight (knock three times on the window and tell them you're a friend of Mick), you'll find it full of freedom fighters, bravely holding out against Dublin rule.

> **If you enter a pub in rural Ireland after midnight you'll find it full of freedom fighters, bravely holding out against Dublin rule.**

Petty crime in Ireland is often committed by drug addicts who need to feed their habits. Organised crime is generally related to drug dealing. But really organised crime tends to be the work of former republican paramilitaries with time on their hands following the ceasefires in Northern Ireland. When a gang stole a record £26 million in a bank robbery in Belfast in 2004, even the dogs in the street knew it was the IRA. Needless to say, they thought twice about barking.

Irish time

It used to be said that the Irish had a relaxed attitude to time. In the era of the Celtic Tiger, this is no longer quite true. Those who spend several hours a day commuting through traffic jams are not very relaxed about it at all. But it is still true to say that, outside of certain formal occasions, the Irish regard an attachment to punctuality as a personality disorder.

Events in Ireland are usually fixed in Greenwich Mean Time. Ireland is some way west of Greenwich, however, so people make their own local adjustments. When it's 1 p.m. in Greenwich, it's still only about 12.30 in Irish real time (eastern zone). You might want to bear this in mind when making lunch arrangements. It follows that the further West you go, the greater the time lag. In parts of Galway, it's still yesterday.

> **The further West you go, the greater the time lag. In parts of Galway, it's still yesterday.**

In general, the Irish are not particularly interested in time. Just ask barmen, who try to introduce the subject for discussion every night. "Time, gentlemen, please," they plead. But customers never show any interest in the topic, and barmen invariably have to broaden the debate to other subjects, such as the classic: "Have yiz no homes to go to?"

The Author

Frank McNally was born close to the border between Ireland's two political jurisdictions, a fact that puts him in the unique position of being equally distrusted by people on both sides. He grew up on a farm, but as with many young men, there came a time when he could no longer resist the lure of the big city. Unable to find one in Ireland, however, he moved to Dublin.

Shrewdly, he spent much of the depressed 1980s working for the unemployment section of the Department of Social Welfare. It was an exciting time for welfare in Ireland, with record growth in all the main schemes. But it couldn't last. By the end of the decade, it was clear the glory days were over.

He left the civil service and spent some time travelling, hoping to find himself. Sure enough, while on a visit to Thailand, he found himself short of money and needing to go home and get a proper job. He turned to journalism, where he learned to cut a long story short. He now works for *The Irish Times*, for which he writes on subjects including parliament, the peace process, and the annual invasion of his kitchen by ants.

The Spanish

Anyone attempting to understand the Spanish must first of all recognise the fact that they do not consider anything important except total enjoyment. If it is not enjoyable it will be ignored.

The Germans

All Germans love to point out to you what you are doing wrong or what you are failing to do right. Thinking of sneaking through a red light? Don't do it. A hundred Germans will helpfully call out that This Is Not Allowed.

The Aussies

The Aussies are not subtle and neither is their language. They will say what they mean. The problem is that the words they use don't always mean what they say, e.g: bluey – someone who has red hair; itsa bit warm – it is probably 120°F in the shade; that'd be right – I don't believe it either.

The Americans

The American language embraces the bias towards good feelings. Stocks that plummet to half their value aren't losers, they're 'non-performers'. Someone doesn't have a near brush with death; he or she has a 'life-affirming experience'.

The Dutch

Few Dutch people go to church any more, but they don't need to. Inside every Hollander's head is a little pulpit containing a preacher with a wagging finger.

The Czechs

Czech beer is not just a lubricant, it's a source of national pride. One of their best ice hockey full-backs Jan Suchý would fill his water bottle not with an isotonic drink but good old Czech beer and knock back a regular shot or two so he didn't have to strain himself with warm-up exercises.

Comments on other titles

On the series:
"An enlightened series, good natured, witty and useful.   Reviewer of *The European*

The Greeks:
"This book is brilliant! I have read it countless times. Hits the nail on the head. Being Greek, I must admit I have rediscovered myself and have also learned a few things too."   Reader from Greece

The Aussies:
"One gem of a book. Compulsory reading for anyone interested in visiting Australia or living there. Don't look like a stunned mullet, read the guide."   Reader from Germany

The Kiwis:
"A great read. A witty and insightful take on what makes New Zealanders so unique!"
    Reader from Australia

The Icelanders:
Fantastic portrayal of a nation. I'm Icelandic myself and everything this book states is completely correct and a greatly humorous view of the nation."

    Reader from Iceland

Xenophobe's® guides

Xenophobe's® lingo learners

"Speak the lingo by speaking English."

Oval Books

5 St John's Buildings   Canterbury Crescent   London SW9 7QH

We like to hear from our readers.
Please send us your views on our books and
we will publish them as appropriate on our
web site: ovalbooks.com.

Oval Books also publish the best-selling
Bluffer's Guide® series –
see www.ovalbooks.com

Both series can be bought via Amazon or directly
from us, Oval Books through our web site
www.ovalbooks.com or by contacting us.

Oval Books charges the full cover price
for its books (because they're worth it) and
£2.00 for postage and packing on the first
book. Buy a second book or more and
postage and packing will be entirely FREE.

To order by post please fill out the accompanying
order form and send to:
Oval Books
5 St John's Buildings
Canterbury Crescent
London SW9 7QH

cheques should be made payable to: Oval Books

or phone us on +44 (0)20 7733 8585
or visit our web site at: www.ovalbooks.com

Payment may be made by Visa or Mastercard and orders are
dispatched as soon as the card details and mailing address are
received. If the mailing address is not the same as the card holder's
address it is necessary to give both.

Oval Books